D1250347

hieroglyphics
of the
heart

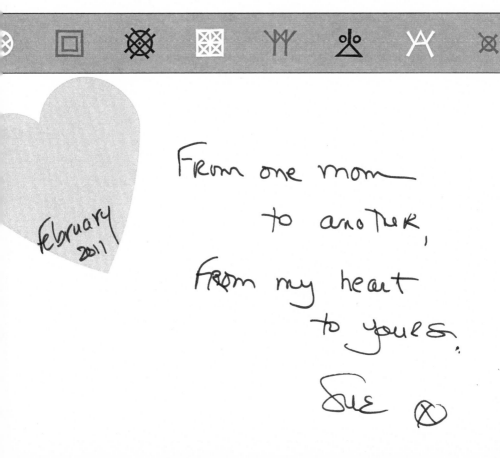

February 2011

From one mom
to another,
From my heart
to yours.

Sue

hieroglyphics
of the
heart

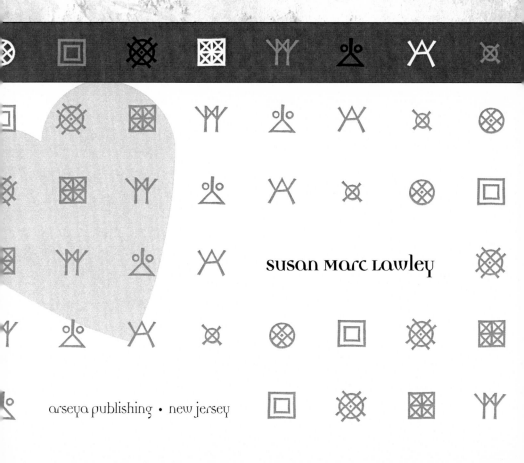

susan marc lawley

arseya publishing • new jersey

Copyright © 2011 by Susan Marc Lawley

All rights reserved.

No part of this book may be reproduced, stored in a retrieval system, or transmitted in any form by any means, electronic, mechanical, photocopying, recording, scanning, or otherwise, without prior written permission except in the case of brief quotations embodied in articles and reviews. For more information contact the publisher at arseya@arseya.com.

Library of Congress Control Number: 2010917687

ISBN-13   978-1-935093-03-9

Cover and text design by Curtis Tow Graphics, New York, NY
Author photo by Donna Blakely
Cover photo by Leslie Willmott

Printed in the United States by The Wall Street Group, Inc., Jersey City, NJ

Published by Arseya Publishing
New Vernon, New Jersey
www.arseya.com

FIRST EDITION

For my parents
who taught me to love;

To my husband Bob,
who makes me feel loved every day;

And our children
who prove the power of unconditional love.

saturated with story

My grandfather's clams
on the half-shell eating contest;
why the outcome proves
he was a good man.

The hazards of going out
in the evening for an ice cream
cone; someone dear
to me is not forgotten.

The rabbit hole of my mother's
recipe box, how creativity
can be found between cannelloni
and custard filling for cream puffs.

Then there's Henrietta,
the baby chick that lived
for five months
in our claw foot tub,
carried to the kitchen sink
every time one of us took a bath.

The secrets of vintage
photographs, antique
apron pockets,
chipped gravy boats.

Memories flood in,
stories flow out.

We are saturated with story.

table of contents

joy

I

On Taking an Old-Fashioned Photo at the Danbury State Fair   2
How to Raise a Boy   4
How to Love a Mom   6
Portrait   8
Bookends   10
Clams on the Half-Shell Eating Contest   12
Blessings I   16
Blessings II   17
Eighty Four Charles Street   18
Still Life: March 9th   20
The Rooster in the Claw Foot Tub   22

heartache

25

Answers   26
Celebration of Life   28
Diagnosis   29

Unsaid	30
Domino Effect	32
Rapid Succession	34
The Choreography of Healing	36
The Great Debate	39
Incantation I	41
Incantation II	42
Funeral Lessons	44
Birthday Girl Bartender	47

hearth   51

Greenwich Village, 1950	52
Under Construction	54
Showing the House I	55
Dialogue with My House (Camelot Manor)	58
Showing the House II	63
Façade	66
156 Doors — Living in a Condominium	68
A Queen Leaves Her Queendom	70

musings   73

Retrievals	74
Stillness	75
Reconfiguration	76
Relinquishment	77
When Artists Go to the Movies	78
Farewell to Belle-Aire	79
Trumps	81
Audacious	83
One Day Older	84
Forgiveness	87

delight

89

Dialogue with a Photograph   90
Phantom Photo   92
Lasting Connections   94
My Father's Eye Loop   96
Thanksgiving   97
A Christmas Kindness   99
My True New Year   101

ACKNOWLEDGEMENTS   103
Full Circle   104
ABOUT THE AUTHOR   106
PRAISE FOR "HIEROGLYPHICS OF THE HEART"   107

joy

on taking an old-fashioned

We are imposters in our own lives.
Donning clothing from another era,
we pose in front of the camera,
hoping for a reverse process.
Perhaps the flash of the bulb
can expose our future,
imprint the years ahead
on the instant at hand.

Will this relationship endure?
We are not touching,
but passion is our only bond.

We look straight ahead,
no glancing back,
no turn of the head,
no remorse for those
we left behind.

photo at the danbury state fair

how to raise a boy

Do not cut the crust
off his sandwiches;
it will make him weak.

Put a note in his lunch bag
but never decorate the outside
with hearts and flowers
or hugs and kisses.
Teach him discretion.

Cherish every gift,
no matter how humble.
Put those five crumpled leaves
in your best crystal vase.
Let him know the joy of giving
by being an enthused recipient
of his offerings.

Arrange his fruit in patterns
on his breakfast plate
so he will start each day
surprised by simple pleasures.

Teach him to cook
and he will feel at home
in any situation.

Study his life; encourage him
to have friends of all kinds.
Better yet, have an interesting
circle of friends yourself.

Honor his father.
Discuss his mother.

Stay up late at night
when everyone else
is in bed
and chat.

Teach him to laugh;
mirth fills the belly.

Allow him to cry.

Know that it was worth it.

how to love a mom

Do not lie to her;
it will make her mad.

Put a frog in her purse
when she isn't looking
but never, I mean never,
bring insects into the house.
Spare her unnecessary shocks.

Convince her to catch lightning
bugs at dusk. Show her the magic
in the world when she is too busy
to see it.

Treasure every argument
no matter how trivial.
Put all her worries
in your hip pocket.
It's the best insurance policy
you will ever have.

Decorate her fridge
with chocolate pudding
portraits so she can work
surrounded by beauty.

Coax her to rollerblade
and she will remember
the feeling of flying
even when you are apart.

Study her past,
see what she was like
when she was your age.

Or drift into her kitchen.
Lick the batter from the bowl.
Eat raw cookie dough.
Steal the crust
from her home-baked pies.

Honor your promises.
Discover your possibilities.

Stay up late at night
when everyone else is in bed
and brew her a cup of tea.

Teach her to trust you
by always being truthful.

Allow her to let you go
by staying in touch every day.

Know that she will always be there.

portrait

She thought it was her fault,
her parents' broken marriage.

Golden-haired girl, transformed
from child to subject of debate,
from daughter to fought-over
companion of each parent.

No longer safe,
       no longer certain,
              no longer smiling,
she exchanged unity for divided holidays,
confidence for competing loyalties.

She was at a formative stage
when her foundation crumbled.
Not yet eight, she wandered
through fourth grade.

Math eluded her:
       1 parent + 1 parent did not equal 2.
Words failed; what did family mean?
It would take a lifetime
to answer these questions.

Music haunted;
melody had become
dirge. Her heart
no longer sang.

But art saved her.
With pen to paper,
paint to canvas,
ink to parchment,
she recreated herself
with images, colors, forms.

She felt chaos,
and found solace
in shaping it
to suit her self.

bookends

My husband bookends
my day with kindness.

Before my eyes open,
he comes with his offering:
hot coffee with cream,
just the way I crave it.

He makes the bed
while I stand in my closet
wondering what to wear.
He turns to perfecting
the hospital corner
while I focus on not focusing
on my imperfections.

Nourished, I move into my work
day, able to rewrite the script
for the publishing president
who has run out of story lines.

I absorb the chaotic energy
of the technology engineer
caught in an endless
circuit of despair.

I redirect the efforts
of a non-practicing attorney
about to object to his own life.

I compute probabilities
for the actuary unable
to forecast his future.

I come home in the evening
to a glass of wine
and dinner cooked
and served without fanfare.

My husband bookends
my day with kindness.

clams on the half-shell eating contest

Circa 1932, Greenwich Village, New York City

The *Hornswoggler Bushwackers* threw out a challenge:
could anyone eat 100 clams on the half-shell?

Coney Island had a hot dog eating contest since 1916;
why shouldn't they have a competition of their own?

Six young men agreed to the dare.
Each put five dollars in bills or coins
in the hands of Heenie the banker.

The seafood peddler on the corner
of Bleecker and Carmine hosted
the event on Friday night.
He'd shucked 30 dozen that afternoon,
put them on ice, ready for the excitement.

The men gathered around the wooden pushcart,
each taking a spot near the ledge where the clams
were on show, along with lemon wedges,
horseradish and hot sauce.

Carlo blew the whistle; slurping overtook
the noise of the traffic. Empty shells
were tossed in a bowl on the counter;
each clang spurred the men on.

After a few rounds, some fell away.
Ernie the barber surrendered to the salty brine.
Jerry "the Deuce" gave up at 47 clams.

My grandfather Bernie, Vito, Danny and Sal
continued eating. All of them made it to seventy-five.

Sal sat on the curb and rested his head;
the others soldiered on.

Danny choked on a fragment of shell,
stopped the action for five full minutes.

Now Bernie began to believe he could win the dare.
His appetite had no bounds, but then he thought
about these families, his neighbors, his friends.
None of them could afford to lose
five dollars, with 13 million out of work,
unemployment near 25%.

And those who had jobs
suffered pay cuts
or a loss of hours
each week.

The Deuce couldn't afford it;
his wife had just given birth.
More mouths to feed.

Sal had lost his job; it might be months
before he could find a new one.
Losing five dollars would set him back.

Danny's wife had a heart condition;
medicine was expensive, the doctor's bills
constantly growing.

But then Bernie thought of Jennie,
his bride and the bright light in his life.
Jennie loved the movies; Radio City
had just opened uptown.
With $30 dollars in his pocket,
they could have a night on the town.

He swallowed more slowly.
He and Vito were up to 92 clams each,
Vito, his best friend, devoted to his mother.
Every spare quarter went to heat
her cold apartment.

At 96, Vito quit. Bernie had 4 more clams
to go to claim the jackpot. He swallowed
a cherrystone.

Now he was facing number 98.
The chanting began,
98, 98, Bernie ate 98.

Bernie looked around; his friends
were waiting to celebrate his win.

But he knew the cost would be too great.
So he ate that 99th littleneck,
and feigned fullness,
patting his midsection,
saying *not another bite.*

The banker returned the money.
They insisted on paying for Bernie's
clams, and he accepted their generosity.

As the group broke up, Bernie smiled.
He knew Jennie had spaghetti and scungilli
simmering on the stovetop.
He slipped into the apartment, sat at the kitchen
table, and piled her food high onto his plate.

The *Hornswoggler Bushwackers* was the
name of a local men's club in Greenwich Village.

blessings 1

(After Stanley Kunitz)

Bless Romolo Marcucci, one of the "four jewels,"
siblings, thriving in their 70s and 80s.

Bless Romolo, who went to work in the Navy Yards
so his two sisters could go to college,
a rarity for women in those days.

Bless Romolo, a World War II vet, who enlisted
so his older brother, Americus, about to have a son,
would be exempted from service.

Bless Romolo, resident of Greenwich Village,
living in a rent-controlled apartment
for more than 50 years,
paying $600 for five rooms,
and complaining about the last $8 increase.

Bless him at age 85,
and keep him safe.

blessings II

(After Stanley Kunitz)

Bless Caterena Teresa Giacalone Marcucci,
first-born of three to Johanna and Bernie.
Her parents, both raised in an orphanage,
married at 15 and 16 to escape its harshness.

Bless this mother of three
who buried her ambition
in the bottom
of the kitchen cupboard,
who traded her desire
to become a doctor
for pride in her elder
son's accomplishments.

He sat with her,
heard her last breaths
in the corner bed
of the ICU
at Memorial Sloan Kettering.

eighty four charles street

1950
Faceted glass doorknobs,
claw footed tub,
gas powered refrigerator:

a gem of an apartment.

1961
Upright piano hoisted through window,
fire escape used as overflow pantry,
pasta drying on chair backs and bedspreads:

christening party, Italian-American style.

1975
Hare Krishnas chant on corners,
Lawrence Welk in black and white.
Failed marriage sends me back.

You can go home again.

1980
Toddler climbs 36 steps
to Grandma's apartment.
Dominoes slide across the linoleum.
Black dots connect ivory rectangles.

Laughter lifts heavy hearts.

1991
The toilet seat is up,
crumbs behind the toaster.
Wrinkled shirts in closet
with missing door.

Dad has been alone a long time.

2005
Crime is down.
Levees collapse.
Tsunami devastates.
Terry Shiavo is unplugged.
London buses explode.

Dad falls down 12 marble steps;
fractures neck.

2009
50 years of rent control over.
Sort personal effects.
Make peace with the past.

Lock the door for the last time.

still life: march 9th

Brown melamine bowl no longer holds fruit,
just a stray religious medal neither silver
nor depicting any favorite saint, precious
because it was given to him
by his long time companion, Josephine.

He used a thick black marker to blot
his name from the mail before discarding.
Page-a-day calendar turned to today,
March 9th, 2009. All the earlier days
stacked neatly next to the pills.

AARP magazine and two-day-old *Daily News*
purchased on the last sunny day of the week.

Old telephone book pops open
to a lettered page depending on
where you place the arrow,
positioned at letter G.

Inside the book, crossed out
numbers and addresses
written in his scribble.

A photo of five couples
in a Lucite frame;
a photo with a story

which my father invented.
Three in the bottom row passed;
he was the only one left.

"You see" he said, "They all went in order.
Looks like I may be next."

I never believed it;
Dad had too much vigor.
But he was tormented
by that image, left it in view.

Finally another friend in the photo
was struck down. The curse curved
around him; the spell was broken . . .

until today.

the rooster in
the claw foot tub

The first clue was the beak sticking out
of the pocket of his brown leather jacket.

In the kitchen, a negotiation began
between the exhausted med student
and our exasperated mother.

The chick changed hands
during their exchange.

My brother took off his scrubs
and retreated to his bedroom
to hit the books; it was exam week.

Our mother took the baby chick
and placed it in the claw foot tub,
then searched the vegetable bin
for wilted spinach leaves
and kernels of corn.

For the next few weeks,
I did my homework accompanied
by the sounds of chirping
and peck peck pecking
on the walls of the tub.

In a couple of weeks,
Henrietta became a fixture
in our family.

Housed in a 450 square foot apartment:
a family of five, one dog
and a newly rescued chick
from the med school lab.

Soon the five plus the fowl
fell into a rhythm.

Each night as one of us
took a bath, our mother
carried Henrietta from the tub
to the kitchen sink
where her pecking was rewarded
with the scraps trapped in the drain.
When we were washed, dried
and revived, the chick was carried back
to the confines of her cast iron coop.

And then, a few months later,
one morning, Henrietta
woke us at 5 am
with a shrill crow.

And had to be renamed.
Henry was not meant
for apartment living
with nineteen other families.

After four days of crowing
and complaints from our neighbors,
Dad, Richard and Henry took a walk
to the pet store near the church.

The proprietor
promised to find
a home for Henry,

who ended up on a farm
in Pennsylvania.

But though he was gone,
none of us ever forgot
the rooster in the claw foot tub.

heartache

answers

(After Mark Strand)
For our Vietnam veterans

Why won't you ever speak of your time in Vietnam?
Because I want to forget.

Why won't you ever speak of your time in Vietnam?
Because I can never forget and it's too painful to remember.

Were you afraid of dying?
No, I was not afraid of dying.
I was young and strong.
I knew I would survive.

Were you afraid of dying?
No, I was not afraid of dying.
I was terrified of not surviving
intact. Losing a limb
or my mind.

Why haven't you stayed in touch with your battalion?
That chapter is closed.
I will not dwell in the past.

Why haven't you stayed in touch with your battalion?
It is better not to know who perished, who suffers still.
My trunk of guilt is under lock and key.

Did you ever kill anyone?
Yes, I killed many,
but I never saw their faces.

Did you ever kill anyone?
Yes, I killed many,
and each face haunts me every day.

Have the horrors of war stayed with you?
I have banished them,
pierced them with my bayonet,
shot them with my rifle,
stunned them with my grenades.

Have the horrors of war stayed with you?
Trucks backfiring in the street startle me.
Rustling leaves make me uneasy.
I relock every door three times
before I go to bed.

Will you ever forgive yourself?
It's not mine to forgive.

It's not yours to forgive?
>   *It is not mine to forgive.*

celebration of life

for MM

A surprise gathering planned for his special day,
friends and family, far and near, gathered at his side.
The evening, marker of their love, celebration of his life.
She toasted him, wished him the things that made him happiest.

Friends and family, far and near gathered at his side.
"It's the hand we've been dealt; we must make the most of this time."
She toasted him, wished him the things that made him happiest.
A week elapsed; a lifetime vaporized before her eyes.

"It's the hand we've been dealt; we must make the most of this time."
Without symptoms, a healthy man transformed to a dying one.
A week elapsed; a lifetime vaporized before her eyes.
We need to pray. Ache for good news.

Without symptoms, a healthy man transformed to dying.
A surprise gathering planned for his special day.
We need to pray. Ache for good news.
The evening, marker of love, celebration of life.

diagnosis
for AM

"That's a bummer," he whispered
to his wife standing at his bedside.
Their future on hold, eyes filled with tears.
The doctor delivered the dreadful news.

To his wife standing at his bedside
he forced his brilliant smile.
The doctor delivered the dreadful news
and, breaking protocol, hugged his patient/friend.

He forced his brilliant smile,
afraid to look beyond this moment.
And breaking protocol, hugged his doctor/friend.
Friends and family, far and near, gathered at his side.

Afraid to look beyond this moment to the next,
"That's a bummer," he whispered.
Friends and family, far and near, gathered at his side.
The future on hold, eyes filled with tears.

unsaid

My mother didn't say "I love you" every day.
She tried to show it instead.

She never wanted anything for herself.
The rare luxury had to be forced on her.
She was content with so little.

My mother failed to mention plans for herself.
They got folded in with her children's plans
like sugar into butter in cake batter.

They were there all the time but invisible,
suspended just below the surface.

To find her desires
you had to dive deep
when she wasn't looking
and trap them
like lobsters scurrying
out to sea.

My mother did not say goodbye
to me at the end.
She could no longer speak.

The breathing machine
stole her voice
like an overprotective parent
pockets the independent spirit
of a child.

She said goodbye to me
with her eyes.
Those lavender eyes
stared intently at me,
and said it all in silence.

domino effect

Our mothers topple like dominoes
set in a measured design.

First Ina, then Catherine,
next Gladys and Irma.

The mere mention of their names
reveals their era,
and with each passing
certain things fall away:

starched lace curtains,
white gloves and girdles,
cut glass crystal,
hand written letters.

A generation vanishes;
images endure:

afternoons at the piano,
walks in a Shelton stroller,
kneeling at the bedside,
hands clasped, head bowed.

Three daughters advance
into the void
their mothers leave.
A place where the current
becomes quaint.

We wonder who will:

wear white cotton nightgowns,
fill teacups with tears,
claim printed words on the page.

The dominoes lean into each another.
Faith travels down the line.
Love and hope remain.

rapid succession

They disappear like sandcastles
caught in the sweep of a wave.
First Heenie, then Catherine,
next Lucia and Salvatore.

My mother is among this set,
five couples captured
in a photograph
decades ago.

My father is the only one
not looking at the camera.
Instead he gazes at his wife
aware their time is ebbing.

Years later,
it is my father who falters,
giving up in rapid succession
the beach house, his car,
long walks to Herald Square.

And with each relinquishment,
I feel myself fade
away, less
than I was yesterday.

Until I turn,
unwilling
to be
his sacrificial offering.

the choreography
of healing

His scuffed slippers drag across the floor
as he follows the therapist's lead,
"Place your walker first, then your bad leg,
now move your right."
This choreography of healing
is accompanied by the click of metal,
then drag and step.

It is an effort to walk these few steps,
but the effect carries me back
almost 50 years.

Click, drag, step

> I see Dad's polished oxfords,
> the vinyl 45 circling slowly
> on the Victrola.
> "Place your feet on mine,"
> he tells me.

> I raise my tiny feet
> and place them on top
> of my father's 9 1/2 shoes.
> He guides me softly:
> *Step, step, glide.*
> *Right, back, left.*

This is magical,
our first dance
across Grandma's
checkerboard linoleum.

Click, drag, step

I see my father's sky blue sneakers
running alongside
my Schwinn three-speed
up and down Temple Avenue.

I hear his voice with every rotation
of the silver spokes.
He shouts "Keep going.
Hold the handle bars steady."
His voice trails off
until all I hear is a whisper
in the wind.

Click, drag, step

I see my father's patent leather slip-ons
reflecting the pressed crease
of his tuxedo pants.

He joins me in the back of the chapel
and walks me down the aisle,
leading me to the elegant Englishman
he never thought would marry me.

And once the party is in full swing
we are dancing again,
three pairs of fathers and daughters:
my radiant mother and proud grandpa,
my mystified father and me,
my handsome husband
and seven-year-old Sharon.

A three generational swirl
of emotion takes the floor
and the tune *You are so beautiful*
echoes in the pale blue ballroom.

When the music stops,
he escorts me to the head table,
bows in front of me and says,
"Thank you for the pleasure of that dance."

Click, drag, step

Now the nurse directs
my weary father
back to his hospital bed.
I tuck him in,
lean and kiss his forehead,
and silently thank him for guiding me
through this waltz called life.

the great debate

The important thing is
that he should not fall again.
Her brother, the doctor, warns
the next one could be devastating.

He's frail but still drags himself
up those four flights of stairs every day.
What's crucial to him is
that he can still do it.

Her younger brother thinks their father
should be moved to assisted living
and has scouted out some places.
"It will improve his social life,"
 her sister-in-law chimes in,
"He will make new friends."
Most of the old ones are gone now.

Her husband thinks he should have an operation.
"What counts now," he says," is quality of life."
"Dad, you probably have ten years left. Do you
want to be sitting in your chair all that time?"

This conversation horrifies her.
It's not that she disagrees.
She hates the idea
that there's only ten years left.

Most essential to her
is that her father make
his own decision, live
where he wants,
has freedom of choice.

Unlike the mama bird who pushes
her hatchling out of the nest,
she encourages her surviving parent
to stay in his comfort zone.

If flying is born out of loving,
not flying can be, too.

incantation I

The year my father died
a woman campaigned
for the Presidency
of the United States.

The month my father died
banks begged for bailouts.

The week my father died
it snowed
on the first day of spring.

The day my father died
the ban on stem cell research
was lifted.

The hour my father died
our 44th President appeared
on The Tonight Show.

The moment my father died
my world dimmed.

The instant my father died
the music stopped.

incantation II

The year my father died
a woman campaigned
for the Presidency of the United States.

> *He would have voted for her.*
> *He taught me that women can do anything.*

The month my father died
banks begged for bailouts.

> *He would have frowned at this.*
> *We never bought anything we couldn't afford.*

The week my father died
it snowed on the first day of spring.

> *He would have cursed the weather.*
> *I would have urged him to stay home.*

The day my father died
the ban on stem cell research was lifted.

If he had had more time, science might have saved him.
Perhaps it will save me someday.

The hour my father died
our 44th President appeared on The Tonight Show.

He would have watched the entire show.
We would have discussed it the next morning.

The moment my father died
my world dimmed.

This would have made him cry.

The instant my father died
the music stopped.

He is unforgettable.

funeral lessons

Uncle Danny's funeral:
sparse hair on satin pillow,
black rosary beads threaded
around his hand with the one cracked
fingernail. Aunt Anna weeps
in their apartment,
unable to come to the wake.
She was sure he would outlive her.
My first lesson in the unexpected.

Four years later, Aunt Anna follows.
Mom turns off the radio for three days.
She cries all the time, not cooking, not cleaning.
Except for her sobs, the house is silent.
From then on, I associate music with life.
I vow to never have a day without song.

Grandpa Giacalone.
I kneel at his coffin and see
his sad brown eyes imploring me
to stay a little longer that New Year's Eve.
"Do you have to go already?" haunts me.
Now I linger at every family gathering,
always the last to leave.

Mom's funeral, Perazzo's Funeral Home,
Bleecker Street, the West Village.
She was only 56.
"The good die young."
Four words repeated over and over
at her wake: "The good die young."
My invitation to be bad.

Uncle Bernie, father of six, step-dad to four,
goes out for a drive and an ice cream cone,
never comes home.
It takes me almost 20 years
to taste ice cream again.
I join Mothers Against Drunk Drivers.

Joe, my father-in-law, succumbs
to the coal miner's plight,
lung disease.
My husband's ex comes to the wake.
She wraps her arms around Bob,
tells him she still loves him.
They have been divorced for ten years.
I eradicate regret from my vocabulary.

Uncle Sal, first in our family to be cremated.
The priest at his service proclaims
our bodies are glorified after death.

No matter their final shocking state,
they are restored to brilliance and beauty.
Within days, I sign an Organ Donor card.

Aunt Laura, 87 years old,
detoured on her first flight to America
in more than 30 years.
Her British Airlines jet lands in Gander,
Newfoundland on 9/11/01.

Sleeping on a cot for three nights,
she treats inconvenience as adventure,
makes new friends, then is whisked back
to Yorkshire when the air space opens.

She never sets foot on American soil,
never visits her younger sister.
The trip, rescheduled for the spring,
never comes, a heart ailment claims her first.

We travel to the north of England
to pay our respects and I realize
whenever I attend a funeral
I learn how to live.

birthday girl bartender

She drove through the intersection,
never noticing the stop sign.
Leaving the world of work behind,
she was eager to continue celebrating.

> On the other side of town, a good-enough man
> waited for his wife to finish her phone call.
> While she lingered in conversation with their son,
> he sat impatiently in the driver's seat.

Her sweaty hands jerked the steering wheel
as she wove in and out of traffic,
thinking about her friends in the bar who partied with her.
They toasted her with good intentions
and bought her drinks garnished with kind words.

> His arthritic hands clutched the steering wheel
> as he backed out of their driveway.
> Thinking about the son who called,
> they toasted their history together,
> excited about their future.

Between the hours of noon and eight, she consumed
19 drinks, one for every year of her life.
This birthday girl bartender, working on her special day,
indulged her urge for celebration, her need to numb her pain.

Between the two of them, they survived two failed marriages,
and produced ten offspring, six boys and four girls.
He was a retired police officer turned chef,
about to open a trattoria
and realize a life-long dream.

She accelerated well beyond the speed limit,
unaware of her surroundings,
impaired in her judgment,
radio blaring, vision blurred;
she lost track of where she was heading.

They meandered down one road and up the next,
taking the scenic route to their favorite ice cream stand.
As the business of the day melted away,
Bernie and Ellen savored the simple decisions ahead:
one scoop or two, chocolate chip or cherry vanilla.

The young driver sped toward the intersection . . .

where the dessert bound driver paused to look both ways.

Out of nowhere, her Pontiac struck them,
tossed their car through the air
where it rolled over three times
landing on its side.

After the impact,
    one good man was taken,
        one woman's life was shattered,
            ten children were traumatized,

after that murderous moment
when everything was altered but nothing really changed,
Alicia went home by way of the police station,
and poured herself another drink.

hearth

greenwich village, 1950

I.
Pushcart peddlers
on cobblestone streets

Fruits and vegetables
stacked in pyramids

Weight scales sway
in morning's breeze

Mothers in housecoats
Fathers in suits and hats

II.
Canvases on display
Annual Art Show

Malcontents march
under the great arch

Hare Krishnas, white-
robed, hand out leaflets

Bakers, butchers, leather-
workers exercise their craft

Lines are crossed
Identities sought

III.
Bohemian hangout
Cafés and jazz clubs

Literary circles
Brentano's on Fifth

Off-Broadway theater
Circle-in-the-Square

Runaways' haven
I was there

under construction

I am under construction.
Watch me take shape.
Peer into the window of my soul.
See what renovation looks like at mid-life.

I am the draftsman of my own design.
I produce the blueprint, feel free to revise it.
I reconsider my façade
and change the face I offer the world.

I am the architect selecting
fixtures for my future,
choosing power sources to sustain,
collecting water to nourish.

I am the decorator of my domain,
determining the color scheme.
I am the designer who discovers
the artifacts worth displaying.

I am the shaman
who checks the feng shui,
who directs the energy
in an uninterrupted flow.

Like the carpenter in the final stage of her craft,
I must take up the cloth and polish my possibilities.

showing the house I

Here they come, the first group of six,
faces full of expectation
ready to explore every inch.

We start in the basement,
looking into the exercise room,
remembering the weeks
when I was disciplined,
followed by many others
when I hoped to be.

We pass the pool table
where my father and husband
had many a good game.
Dad threatened to win;
Bob usually did.

I open the door to Bob's workshop,
the place where he was going to make
things. On the butcher block counter,
he repaired countless earrings,
broken bowls and chipped figurines.
The vice, however, hangs limply,
never tightened.

We peek into the basement's full bath,
which features a steam shower
used more often to remove the creases
from my son's shirts than to rejuvenate
his body.

On the main level, we move into the laundry
room, remarking on the unusual ceramic tiles,
keeping silent about the story they represent.

The kitchen holds too many memories,
both quick meals and holiday banquets.
And what about the pinochle marathons
played on the table or the games of seven
where strategy and luck converge?

The family room boasts a wood-burning
fireplace. I think about those winter nights
when I would look into those flames,
lose myself in the embers.

Tucked around the other side of the fireplace
is our master bedroom, where we retreated
from the world. The master bath has a Jacuzzi
big enough for two. I count on one hand
the number of times we soaked in that tub.

Upstairs, a trilogy of bedrooms lines the corridor,
each with private bath; at the end of the hall, another door
leads to the cedar closet with blankets, woolens and furs.

I skirt past a storage room which holds unopened
boxes, memories our son never unpacked
after our move to this house,
the one he didn't want to live in
and now hates to leave.

We exit down the back staircase into the garage,
the cleanest, neatest garage in town
which houses the forbidden yellow motorcycle.

In the backyard, we walk through the "park-like setting"
described in the newspaper ad and around the pool
with the mosaic mermaid, our nightly companion
during sunset swims.

To these prospective buyers, I showcase
the grandeur of this house
which reminds me of everything
I love about it.

Why are we selling this treasure?
It's a puzzle to me,
a riddle to be solved
after I pack and move on.

dialogue with my house (camelot manor)

House: Who are these people and what is that metal post sticking up alongside my fence?

Sue: Those are photographers, taking pictures of you from every angle.

House: Oh, I'm going to be in a magazine—is it *Architectural Digest*? Are they doing a spread on me, showing off all my features to their readers?

Sue: Not quite, CM; the photos are to list you on Realtor.com and the multiple listing service. I'm afraid you're for sale.

House: What did you say?! You didn't say "I'm for sale" did you? Not those dreaded words. And you're afraid? Do you have any idea how those words terrify me? A house just never knows who might march through the doors next. I've already had three sets of owners and I'm only 25 years old. I'm not sure I can handle another change; it's too much of an adjustment.

Sue: Don't be silly CM; everything will be fine. We'll go through this transition together. I'll help you.

House: Some help you are. Didn't you just move in? Didn't you tell me I was beautiful and everything you ever wanted in a home? The only thing you needed to make you happy?

Sue: I did, CM, and I meant it, every single word, but now I'm learning that happiness is fleeting.

House: You're telling me. I woke up happy this morning and now this—a photo shoot. What a shock to my system! Didn't I make you as happy as you thought I would?

Sue: In every way possible. You were warm when I needed warmth, cozy when I wanted intimacy. You were a welcome sight to my eyes after being away for any length of time.

House: If that's true, then how can you leave me?

Sue: I will miss you terribly. But it's time to move on.

House: Are you ready?

Sue: I could stay longer. Another two or three years would have suited me fine. But why put us both through that, if the move is inevitable? I feel strong enough now to make it happen.

House: So you're strong now. Suppose I'm not? What would happen if I just crumbled?

Sue: You won't do that, CM. You're solid as a rock, built of the finest materials: stone, brick and glass. And you're too stately to do something foolish. No, you'll stand strong, of that I can be certain.

House: What can I be certain about any more? People come and go. They settle into me and then just as we're getting comfortable with each other, they move on. It makes no sense at all.

Sue: So much in life is inexplicable, CM. I don't have the answers.

House: You have to explain it. I can't go on without understanding why this is happening. I need to know what I have to do differently so that good people will stay.

Sue: You must stay true to yourself and live in the moment. Enjoy people while they're with you. Don't relive the past and don't fret about the future. In the end, life is composed only of those moments in which we pay attention.

House: Don't fret! Are you kidding? I feel frantic. I want a plan, something I can dig my foundation into. I want to know what lies around the corner. I want to prepare.

Sue: Life is unpredictable, CM. The thrill is in not knowing what lies around the bend.

House: Now they're taking photos of my backside. You know that's not flattering. Tell them to stop. They've been at it for 40 minutes; enough already.

Sue: They have no intention of stopping; in fact, in a few minutes, they'll be coming inside.

House: Absolutely not. I'm in no condition for company. I'm too upset. Tell them to come back another day.

Sue: Take it easy; you're always ready for company. You are the neatest house in town. Our friends say no one lives here; you're too clean. Wouldn't it be nice to be a little bit messy once in a while? To let your guard down?

House: I guess so; I haven't been able to relax in a long time.

Sue: That's more like it. Let's calm down and remember the good parts.

House: Were there bad bits then?

Sue: See what I mean? You are so uptight! Many more good than bad, that's for sure.

House: So let's discuss the good. What do you like best about me?

Sue: I love your substance and your personality. Not only do you have curb appeal, but you have interior heart and soul. Anyone who walks through your doors feels welcome and safe.

House: Did you have good times within my walls?

Sue: Some of the best of my life. Parties galore. Moments on the back patio sipping coffee, watching the birds and reading poetry or trying to write. Lingering mornings. But there were bittersweet moments, too, like when I had to launch my son off to law school. I still have separation anxiety.

House: I think that's what I'll be suffering from when you leave.

Sue: I can't deny it; it's not a great feeling. But we will always be connected and you will always be my favorite house. Maybe I'll write about you in one of my stories.

House: Can you think of one day that you'll never forget?

Sue: Oh, there are several, but September 11, 2001 is the most memorable. All four of us were glued to the television set for hours, making frantic phone calls to locate our relatives in transit from the North of England to JFK. Another day was watching the election returns in November of the previous year, going to bed thinking one man would be President, only to wake and find another man claimed the office. I wonder where I'll be watching the election results this November.

House: And I can't imagine who will be here doing the same. It's unsettling. Let's change the subject. Name one thing that surprised you about me.

Sue: I never knew until recently how your front doors sparkle whenever a car's head lights approach them, and how they glimmer when the tail lights depart the property.

House: Think about that, Sue. That image will be my final glimpse of you, a ruby view as your car leaves the property for the last time.

Sue: Did you know the ruby signifies love and passion? In China, red is the color of good luck, and in Russia, red means beautiful.

House: How fitting!

showing the house II

They come in waves crashing on our leaded glass
shores, a steady and unending flow of people
streaming into our midst.

Four groups already in one day.
The process is wearying after only
one week. Our dog barks, defends our turf.
We concentrate hard, trying to spot
true buyers from the passers-through.

The first couple lives in our town,
about our age. They're impressed
with the property and what we've done with it,
polite and charming when they say their goodbyes.
I want to run after them, tell them not to buy our house,
it's too big, their children are grown, they don't need it.
But I close the door, hoping they've already realized this.

The next group of three generations waltzes in
without acknowledgment, traipsing as though
they already live here. The oldest daughter
bangs the keys on my piano; her parents
do not chastise her. The discordant notes
match my mood, a disturbing
lack of harmony creeps in.

The next couple looks far too young to buy this house.
The husband, not much older than our son, is full
of questions about how the house was built.
His final query seals his fate: how much
are the monthly utilities? That's like asking
the price of gasoline when buying a yacht.
I rule them out instantly.

Finally, at day's end, a ray of hope.
A couple, both lawyers, enter our home;
the husband knows our son. Now we stand
on common ground. The wife recognizes
a painting in one bedroom; she went to school
with the artist, a family friend. Her mother says
she remembers me from her dry cleaning shop,
when my career was in full swing.
Her father notices Cousin Brucie's
signature on a framed photograph;
he is a fan.

These points of connection encourage me.
Could this be the family worthy of Camelot
Manor? This jewel of a house I am forsaking;
I mean, vacating? Might these be the ones
who will watch election returns
in November inside these walls?

They have two children, but did not bring them
on this visit. I see this home filled up again,
every bedroom occupied, legal briefs spread
across a desk, toys and clothes strewn
about the children's rooms. This stately home
will be messy, lived in.

The couple thanks us for showing them our house.
As their car exits the gated entry, their tail lights
reflect on our front doors bouncing ruby rays
around the family room.

I am left with a ruby view,
and, for the first time,
see myself packing and moving on.

façade

I've never missed our house since we moved,
the grand estate I named *Camelot Manor*.
I thought I would be distraught for months,
But in a funny way, I feel free.

The house, situated in a park-like setting
in the center of our town boasted
electrified gates, 16 rooms, 4 garages,
a swimming pool. It was magnificent,
stately, an imposing presence.

When I met people in the supermarket
who asked me where I lived,
I would say, across from the library,
the brick and stucco house.

They would look at me astonished.
"Are you talking about the house on the curve?
The one with the black wrought iron fence?"

"Yes," I would reply, and then the conversation
would focus solely on the house,
the manicured lawns, the lavish rose garden.

And as the house loomed larger,
I became smaller; I could hardly
remember my own name.

I needed something inconspicuous,
so that people could connect to me,
and discover what I'm made of.

We moved into an active adult community
where all 156 units are exactly the same.

So now the distinguishing features
will have to be my own.

156 doors—
living in a condominium

I pledge allegiance to 1 flag of the United States of America,
and to the community with 4 umbrella stands,
one nation, under G_d, whose name is written on parchment,
curled into 22 Mezuzahs and placed on doorjambs.

The Four Seasons, a neighborhood decorated
with 42 floral wreaths, offering liberty and justice to all.

All, that is, except for the resident in Unit 310.
This 60's activist, folk singer and grandmother
to a multicultural clan has posted an anti-war
poster on the outside of her front door.

James Brown sang, "War, what is it good for?
Absolutely nothing, say it again."
The Master Deed, section 11.04, clearly states,
"No signs may be displayed in common areas."

Her neighbor, a WWII vet, is offended by the poster.
The peaceful environment in Building Three is broken.
If you seek peace in condo living, take down your signs.

The American flag draped across the door of Unit 209
stays in place; that display protected by law.

I mourn the loss of freedom of speech
in our community; I am silenced
by this conformity.

I turn my attention
to one stone bunny, two ceramic angels,
and a metal horse posed in mid-
gallop in front of Unit 504.

In numerology, 5 + 4 equals completion.
That metal horse completes the circle for me;
she becomes an endangered species.

I shudder to think of that horse shoved
in the back of someone's closet, her mane
tangled up with starched shirt sleeves, forgotten
scarves, out-of-date neckties.

Instead, I see her prancing through the breeze
in an open meadow where there are no rules
to follow, no regulations to enforce.

a queen leaves
her queendom

I once had a home that was grand,
16 rooms, electrified gates, a swimming
pool with a mosaic mermaid.
I left it all behind for the love of a man.

I once had an impressive job,
complete with power and prestige,
expense accounts and first class travel.
I left it all behind for the love of my boy.

I once had a son
who grew tall and straight,
who stayed up late to make me laugh.
He left it all behind for his love of the law.

I once had a company of my own,
my Queendom called Camelot;
a place where everyone was equal
and all were treasured.
I left it all behind for the sake of a brother.

I once had a mother dear
who taught me to cook,
passed on her recipe for joy.
She left us all behind.

But we have gathered since:
the man I love,
the boy I miss,
the brother I toiled beside.

And we link our arms
around the father we cherish
to protect him from the fall.

As the Queen who left her Queendom
behind, I feel more regal than I ever did
in ermine robes.

I feel something more precious
than crown jewels.

I feel useful in the world.

musings

retrievals

What am I looking for?
    The counsel of a mother lost when I was 30,
    toddler in tow, life in simpler times,
    little money, few possessions,
    my younger self, unwrinkled, unafraid.

What am I searching for?
    The counsel of the universe,
    the lessons of the stars,
    the challenge of living simply
    in a complicated world,
    how to find my truest self.

What am I waiting for?
    the right moment,
    the perfect time,
    the opportune place,
    the alignment of the stars.

What have I discovered?
    My mother sits before me
    in the image of that toddler,
    now 30. My face with its wrinkles
    is the unpretentious version.
    Living simply is much more
    complicated than it seems.

There is no right moment,
no perfect time, and the stars only align
when there is harmony in my heart.

stillness

I am a stranger to stillness.
uncomfortable in her presence,
fleeing every chance I get.

Born at 4 am on the 5th of July,
daughter to the frenetic,
fathered by a fireworks display,
named Sparkle in the Sky,
I become the nocturnal sun.

My life is a kaleidoscope of activities
in constant motion, never the same way twice.

I am a stranger to stillness,
yet I long to know her gifts:
steadiness,
lack of expectation,
openness.

I slow my pace to search for her,
but she is too silent for my pulsing mind,
too steady for my racing heart.

I journey on, find her accomplice,
the Hammock, slide into its crocheted
caress. I feel the breeze over and under
my clattering spirit.

My head sinks,
pulse slows,
muscles relax,
mind empties.

No longer a stranger to stillness,
answers come to questions
I did not know I had.

reconfiguration

for my clients

I have outgrown my occupation.
Everyday tasks no longer motivate me;
ambitions bulge through each frayed seam.
I pour myself through a funnel of frustration.

Everyday tasks no longer motivate me.
I get claustrophobic surrounded by old notions.
I pour myself through a funnel of frustration,
move mannequin-like through a maze of dead ends.

I get claustrophobic surrounded by old notions.
My head bubbles over with ideas suppressed and shunted.
Moving mannequin-like through a maze of dead ends,
I wiggle out through a hole in my own pocket.

My head bubbles over with ideas suppressed and shunted.
I have outgrown my occupation.
I wiggle out through a hole in my own pocket.
My ambitions bulge through each frayed seam.

relinquishment

Living well imprisons my hands;
I cannot write.
The lap of luxury holds no words
for my starving soul.

I sell my belongings on eBay.
A woman in Oregon buys
my almost-new comforter for $25.
She kisses her son goodbye at the airport.

He flies off to Iraq.
She drives home and collapses
under the silky blue and yellow quilt.
Its softness helps her sleep.

We are connected by comfort,
and I am relieved of my ration
of guilt.

when artists go to the movies

At the cinema,
the musically inclined
turn off their cells phones in unison,
creating a cacophony of ring tones.

Throughout the previews
and lulls in the action,
the painters consult each other
about the slant of light
falling on the silver screen.

And when the credits roll, most leave
but the writers stay, reading
each line,
every word
all the letters
that
scroll
away.

farewell to belle-aire

Today they demolished the neighborhood bowling alley.
The orange shovel swallowed our memories: the neatly stacked
pins, the automatic mechanisms that swept the aisles,
the concession stand, the vintage green and white shoes,
tally pads replaced decades ago by electronic scoreboards.

I see a woman on the corner taking photographs,
and wonder who she is and why she cares.
Is she the owner documenting the death of her business?
A reporter from the local paper marking the changing landscape,
sent on assignment to document the transformation of a busy corner?
With camera in hand, she clicks repeatedly, while the shovel ferries
fragments into the receptacles.

Was she a worker there, displaced by another disruption?
The bowling alley will be replaced by a pharmacy, the fourth
within 50 yards, proof that we would rather nurse our ailments
than strengthen our connections.

Was she a bowling league member who came to Belle-Aire Lanes
each Wednesday night for friendly competition? Maybe she was a member
of the High Scorers Club, a brass plaque bearing her name and best score
hidden in the wreckage.

Why do I care? I haven't bowled in years, don't belong to a league;
my purple monogrammed ball collects dust in the attic.

Why does seeing this demolition stop me in my tracks?
When you approach the corner from the east, one wall
still stands, masking what lies beyond. The façade
reveals nothing of the bleakness around the bend.

Much like my life, the buried dreams,
the forgotten promises, the indefinite plans.

I have a sudden urge to bowl,
to knock down every pin,
to spare no sentiment,
to strike out in a new direction,
to reframe what's left of my life.

trumps

I trade my worries like cards
in a game of draw poker,
toss three into the center,
and retrieve three more,
hoping to better my hand.

I write my fears in the sky
with invisible ink.
When I turn a corner, they reappear
as hieroglyphics in my heart.

I place my anxieties in a pot
with mulling spices.
I stir and strain them,
put the lid on,
let them stew.

I coax my concerns through a crack
in the garden wall.
They overtake the ripening fruit,
deflower the emerging blossoms,
disarm the fragrant herbs.

I send my obsessions underground,
bury them deep in the past,
lock the doors to their future.
They bubble up through the earth,
persist through the years
with geyser-like regularity.

I tack my troubles to the bulletin
board next to my lost receipts,
mat and frame them,
put them up for display.
They can't run away.

I trade my worries like cards in a game of draw poker.
I take an unmatched set and exchange them for a flush.
No pairs, no runs, no fancy tricks,
just five cards connected by color.

I've exchanged shades of suspicion
for one single hue of hope.

audacious

A new calendar sits on my desk.
Square boxes line up
to synchronize the chaos of my life.
365 pristine pages.
I want them to fill them all.

I start by noting birthdays.
In April my father turns 83.
September, my husband deeper in his 60's.

I pencil in our wedding anniversary.
February 11th, the closest Saturday
to Valentine's Day that year.
I never imagine that we might be apart,
that the yellow roses might not come.

I write in my niece's wedding date,
March12th, expecting to be there,
in my new dress, 15 pounds lighter.

I draw lines through the three weeks
when we will cruise the South Pacific,
going through the itinerary in my mind:
Tahiti, Bora Bora, Easter Island.
I take out trip insurance,
but never consider I might not go.

I don't think about the past year,
and its changes. That would be
like letting a wrong turn
ruin an otherwise good trip.

365 days of possibility.
I want them all.
I am greedy for time.

one day older

I try to make it special,
this gift of one more day.

But routine takes over my plans,
chipped away by client needs,
phone calls, meetings,
discussions of fears and dreams.

This day is the day I turn
one day older than my mother
who never lived to see
56 years, 7 months and 10 days.

One afternoon, I sat down
with calendar and calculator to compute
what courage divided by loss equals.

I worked the keypad feverishly
like a master accountant
to calculate her life,
20,663 days.
Today I have one more.

I want to make this day special,
starting with a bath, water temperature
99 degrees, Carole King on the CD player
reminding me *You can do anything*.

I soak until my fingers are as wrinkled
as my husband's unpressed shirts
heaped in the corner. I linger in the steam,
pull the plug; my anxieties circle down the drain.

I eat cold anchovy pizza for breakfast
watch my favorite soap opera,
following the story line of 20 years.
There is comfort in things
that do not change in drastic ways.

When the show starts to tire,
I organize my closets, put loose photos
in albums with captions; write letters
to close friends. I cook a month's
nutritious meals from scratch,
and store them in the freezer.
I finish that scrapbook of my son's achievements,
starting with the *peanut scramble*
in swimming class as a four year old *guppy*.
I listen to voice mail, skipping until I hear
my husband saying *I am the love of his life*
and I rewind this one at least a dozen times.
I plan the guest list and menu for my 35th
anniversary, even though it's four years away.
I watch *Gone with the Wind* twice.

But this fantasy is not how the day turns out.
I do get champagne in the evening,
a glass for Mom and one for me.

I stare at the bubbles
and see the next chapter
of my life burst and pop.

I've come to a fork in the road,
the point where I leave my mother
behind and chart a new course.

This is the day I promised
to remember, etch in my heart,
carve in my mind, stamp
on the passport of my soul.

But February 15th turns out
to be an ordinary day,
a day of simple actions
and fleeting thoughts.
A day when the dog still
needed to be walked,
the mail retrieved and sorted,
the dishes washed and put away.

The kind of day my mother
would have recognized,
and rejoiced in.

forgiveness

Rarely one to turn the other cheek,
I marvel at the Amish who turn the soil
and bury their sorrow in a freshly plowed pasture.

I am catapulted by kindness.
I can do small deeds, carrying
groceries for my neighbor,
staying late when someone
needs to leave early,
but I stand in awe of the grand gesture,
like the "secret Santa" who gives away
$1 million in $100 bills in thrift shops,
parking lots, diners.

I am fascinated by forgiveness,
but able to hold grudges longer
than Mount Etna's endless slow
eruption. I am astonished by a Pope
who faces his alleged assassin
and prays to understand him.

I am mesmerized by mercy.
Sometimes I prematurely judge
or wrongly accuse, but I am struck
by those who defend inmates
on death row, exonerate
an innocent man.

I am fascinated by forgiveness,
yet I'm an injustice collector
who tucks each slight in my backpack
and examines it from every angle,
I am in awe of the mother whose son
is murdered on an Italian highway,
then donates his organs to local children.

I am enchanted by compassion,
inspired by the husband who cares
for his bedridden wife, the child
who empties his piggy bank
to feed the hungry, the doctor
who donates her time
to treat the cancer patient
without insurance.

I am fascinated by forgiveness,
when it veers close to home,
when I must deal with an ungrateful
child, a sarcastic in-law,
the rebuffs of my co-worker,
I turn to stone or a pillar of salt.

Forgiveness is the sun in my life
warming from a distance.
When I invite it closer,
it scorches my wings.

delight

dialogue with a photograph

S. I can't believe you're back after all these years.

P. I had to come. It's a special occasion. How could I stay away and miss the celebration, my only daughter turning 50. By the way, how did I get here?'

S. Funny you should ask, Mom. Through the marvel of modern technology and digital imaging. Bob brought you back with the help of a forensic artist.

P. Bob? The Bob I banished from your life 25 years ago has brought me back?

S. The same. Ironic isn't it? To think you confiscated his photo from under my pillow, and now, years later, he developed this photo of you for my desktop.

P. So how do I look? Am I what you expected?

S. You look a little sad, Mom. And tired. I would have expected a more refreshed look after lounging around heaven all these years.

P. Is that what you think? We just hang out in heaven? I'm sorry to tell you, but I've been busy. I've been given the task of organizing the celestial calendar. It's a hologram: past, present, and future all co-existing on one mega PDA.

S. Mom, you've gotten high tech since I've seen you! What else is different about you? And you never answered why you look sad.

P. Well that should be obvious, darling. We've been apart more than 20 years. I've been missing you. It's nice to be back for a while.

S. What else is different, Mom?

P. I'm pain-free, Sue, no pain where I reside.

S. What do you think is different about me?

P. Not much, Sue. I was hoping to see more. Not that I want to be critical, but you're still doing too much. Still trying to force 10 lbs. into that 5 lb. bag of your life. Didn't I teach you that life is short; you've got to slow down and enjoy it?

S. But I do enjoy it, Mom. The exhilaration, the learning, the people I meet.

P. Yes, darling but you move too fast. It must all be a blur to you. Stop, take a deep breath. Notice the view. You won't be here forever you know. Didn't my short life show you that? So why do you want me back now?

S. I wanted you to see what I've made of myself. I wanted your approval.

P. You have it, Sue, but you really don't need it. You're a remarkable woman; you must know that.

S. It carries more weight coming from you.

P. Funny, Sue. In the afterlife, you have no weight. Like an astronaut, I'm weightless.

⊠

phantom photo

There is a photo on my bookshelf of a woman who
does not exist. Her face is found in a silver frame
placed among the other family photos on my shelves.
She bears a resemblance to others in the family, but
she is not real.

I am approaching my 50th birthday, and my husband
asks me what I want as a gift. I am not aware that
he is planning a huge surprise party. The details have
been in the works for months: invitations, flowers,
musicians. Everything is being arranged, but Bob
wants to get me a special gift. I can think of nothing
I need or want. I give him no clues.

At dinner one evening, I remind Bob that on my
50th birthday, my mother would have been 75.
I wonder what she would look like if she were here
today. I speculate about how she would have aged.

My husband takes the bait I did not realize I was
offering. He searches the internet for a forensic
artist. He finds an artist affiliated with the NYPD.
Stephen and Bob talk over the project, and the artist
tells my husband he needs photos of my mother from
different angles and at different ages. And a photo
or two of her sister would be helpful, plus photos of
their mother.

Bob sets off on a hunt searching for the items on his list. He does this without my knowledge, rummaging through old photo albums when I am out at work or busy in another part of the house. He mails a packet to Stephen and waits.

On the 8th of June, one month before my birthday, Bob seems jittery as we dress to go to dinner with some friends. I notice that my mother-in-law has had her hair done, but think nothing of it. Our son has made himself scarce.

We head off to a friend's restaurant and are greeted by the owner. He escorts us through the lobby and says before we sit down, he'd like to show us how he's redecorated one of the banquet rooms. We head up the stairs and approach two carved oak doors which are pushed open to shouts of *Surprise, Surprise!* My eyes take in a sea of people; as many as 100 are in the room.

After making my way through the countless hellos, hugs and kisses, Bob walks me to our table. At my place setting, facing me in a gilded frame is a photo of the woman who does not exist, my mother at 75.

lasting connections

This letter has passed through
her hands and mine.

She wrote it twice; I have read
it a thousand times.

I wondered why she had to write.
Why she couldn't tell me
her thoughts, hopes, fears?

But in the end, I am grateful
she had this urge
to document her feelings,
submit to paper her thoughts
about each of us.

This piece of paper
means more to me
than anything I own.

It is more important
than my birth certificate,
because it is my true birthright.

It is more valuable
than my social security card,
identifying me in
a meaningful way.

It is more precious
than any diploma,
has educated me
in more enduring ways.

This letter my mother wrote
defines who she was,
suggests who I try to be.

my father's eye loop

is the object I would like to have when he is gone.
He squinted through it every day for more than 40
years, making the needles that cut the grooves
in records. His monotonous task led to music
in the world.

His work involved not just the eye loop,
but a grinding wheel and microscope.
One might mistake him for a scientist in his lab
but my father was more artist than engineer,
more Perry Como than Thomas Edison.

Production relied on rare materials:
precision steel shanks, sapphire tips, diamond
dust. The point of each stylus resembled
praying hands when viewed under magnification,
perfectly symmetrical, flawlessly balanced.

The business boasted 65 people at its height,
and the factory buzzed with activity.

Then, without warning, the industry shifted
from vinyl to eight-track tapes. They didn't see
change coming, production halted.

Just as his children didn't see his impending
departure, six days from diagnosis to demise.

His breathing stopped, no time to prepare.
No more turns of the grindstone.

thanksgiving

When my Grandmother sat at her thanksgiving
table, she embraced her family, her three,
their eleven, mates and friends. Twenty-four
surrounded the rectangular pine table circled
with mismatched chairs, benches and stools.
The lavish food was crafted with love.
The choices were plentiful; we could not
see any fraction of the tabletop, covered
with china plates, tureens and platters.
Chianti flowed from a straw-covered bottle.
Conversation flowed, too. Often, one strand
of chatter would cross over another. Other
times, everyone was riveted to a sole storyteller.

When my mother sat down at her Thanksgiving
table, we said grace. Crowded into our cramped
city apartment were her three children, two
mates, one grandchild and one sibling's family.
Fourteen sat at my mother's round oak table
or at the card table in the living room. So many
courses: antipasto, homemade pasta, turkey,
sausage stuffing, stuffed artichokes, candied yams,
cranberry sauce, roasted nuts, prickly pears
and pumpkin pie. The wine poured from bottles;
conversation poured from those who no longer
saw each other every day.

When I sit at my Thanksgiving table, I clink my glass
with those around me, my husband, father, son, mother-in-law,
a companion, a girlfriend. Seven sit at my table. Traditional
foods are served, but are not consumed with gusto. Almost
as much food leaves the table as is first set down. In recent
years, we've skipped the pasta, so that only half a piece of pie
will be thrown away instead of a whole one. I'll continue
to do this even though I know most of what I cook will not
be eaten. I do it for the ghosts of the past.

When I sit at my Thanksgiving table, I see my dead mother
thanking me for carrying on her traditions, for honoring her
holiday, for remembering her.

When I sit at my Thanksgiving table, I do not see my two
brothers. My older brother, an emergency room doctor, is
often working, treating the injuries of strangers. But there
is no one here who can heal the gaping family wound.
My younger brother is with his wife's family. I hoped we
would alternate, Margaret's family one year, ours the next.
This would add five more people, an even dozen.

I have the matching chairs, missing plates, uneaten food.
I am waiting...

a christmas kindness

I do not know her well,
my client Tina.

Out of work,
      out of sorts,
            out of cash,
four kids at home,
husband's business dwindling.

I am her coach,
      her counselor,
            her confidante,
encouraging her to take the next step forward,
reminding her of her strengths,
challenging her to be daring.

I'm exorcising her doubts, but not my own.

At home, my husband of 25 years,
is deathly ill, recovering from three surgeries
in a row, fevers, infections, trauma.

It is Christmas, but no decorations
adorn our house. Not a single red
and white soldier marches up our drive,
no star tops the fountain in the front yard,
the Christmas village is packed away,
Mary, Joseph and Jesus nowhere in sight.

And worst of all, no Christmas tree.

There has never been a Christmas
without a Fraser fir,
      multi-colored lights,
            ornaments and candy canes.

But this year is different;
Bob has no strength to trim the tree
and having others do it would only
showcase this deficiency.

I am resigned to it,
no Christmas tree this year.

And then one snowy afternoon,
the doorbell rings; a UPS man
hands me a rectangular brown parcel.
The return address is not familiar.

I open the box and lift out
the most exquisite miniature tree
I have ever seen.

At the bottom of the box,
the note reads:
*Enjoy the holidays. Good health
in the New Year.
Love, Tina*

The tiny tree is decorated
with colored lights,
snowmen, gingerbread boys
and red and gold bows.

I place the tree on a table
and plug it in.

My heart lights up.

my true new year

After MR and our blank page

My true New Year is not December 31st
at the stroke of midnight.
When the ball drops and the clock strikes twelve,
I worry about uneven numbers.
Will there be an odd man out tonight,
someone who has no one to hug or kiss?

That happened to my father,
when my mother was laid to rest
one day before the turn of the year.

I went to him at midnight,
held him tight, while my husband,
toddler in his arms,
waited for my embrace.

The day itself, 01-01
is no more festive,
a reminder of all I failed to do
in twelve months prior,
all I have yet to accomplish
in the months and days ahead.

No, 01-01 is just an arbitrary line
dividing disappointment and dread.

My true New Year,
a weekday in mid April,
encompasses a ritual,
a reminder of my mother.

It's a day I don't go to work,
a day I spend among strangers,
having stepped out of my clothes,
I wear a robe
which ties in front.

On this day,
I expose my naked breasts
to a technician and machine
that presses my flesh.
I hold my breath,
not just for the procedure,
but until I get the results.

While the pictures are being
developed, I think of my mother,
claimed by this disease.

I sit alone in a dark space
counting my overlooked blessings.
Then, a knock on the door,
a brief exchange.
Things look fine, Susan.

These four simple words crank
the engine of my life back up.
I have been given 365 more days,
to work, to play,
to do good in the world.

This is my true New Year.

acknowledgements

My love of writing starts with Ms. LaRubio who insisted that I infuse my words with emotion, continues with Terry DiAntonio who served as my first serious critic, gets nurtured by Hannelore Hahn and the IWWG faculty and fellow writers; Julie Maloney and the many brilliant writers of *Women Reading Aloud*, goes deeper with Eunice Scarfe and her blank page, Patricia Lee Lewis and the Amherst Writers and Artists Method, Natalie Goldberg and her meditative offerings, is inspired by the words of Laura Boss, Billy Collins, Maria Mazziotti Gillan, Ted Kooser, Dorianne Laux, Perie Longo, and Charlotte Mandel.

My ideas gain flight once released to my *Sisters-in-Script*, Phyllis Fiarotta and Laura Wilson.

They find serious form when shared with my study buddies — Jodie Morrow and Marie Reilly.

They are artistically arrayed on the page by my role model and confidante, Rosemary McGee.

They are sculpted and polished by my friend and mentor, Barbara Crooker, and with any luck, they will linger in the hearts of my readers.

full circle

I cannot exist without gratitude.
I am grateful to the husband
who stays at home and walks the dog,
while I am here walking through memory.

I am grateful to the friend who comes with me,
who waited five hours in the airport lounge
when I missed my plane connection.

I am grateful to the son
who goes about his day
and does not interrupt my thoughts.
He doesn't call, no message light is lit
except on Sunday to say Happy Mother's Day.

I am grateful to the mother, long since gone,
who taught me the beauty of small celebrations,
the power of ritual, and who told me
Never expect gratitude.
I am rarely disappointed.

I am grateful to the mother-in-law
who dresses as she likes, drives
where she wishes, eats what she pleases.
She models the power of *productive aging*
as I stand on the threshold of her space
and begin to look in.

I am grateful to my Sisters-in-Script
who read and write and tell their stories,
who listen and weep
and encourage my own.

I am grateful to myself for making the resolution
that got me here, for calling to register,
book the tickets, pack the clothes,
pay the bills before I left,
select the pens and pads I took.

I am grateful to still be here,
to find the words,
to shape the stories,
to share my gratitude.

about the author

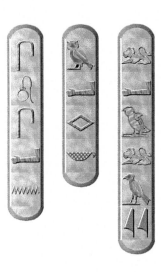

Dr. Susan Marc Lawley is a leadership and life coach, award-winning entrepreneur and inspiring writing instructor. Since 2001, Sue has fashioned her own MFA by attending workshops and master classes with notable poets and writers in stunning locations around the United States.

In 2008, Sue launched *Sisters-in-Script*, a non-profit organization devoted to the professional and personal development of women writers. *Sisters-in-Script* offers writing programs and networking events for women who love to labor with words. Three times a year, Sue offers her *Keepsake Conversations* workshop in which participants bring a treasured memento or family heirloom and write about the object using a six-part model she developed. Since 2009, *Sisters-in-Script* has awarded an annual grant to support an author who wishes to self-publish her debut manuscript. Information about workshops or applications for the self-publishing grant can be obtained by emailing Sue at sistersinscript@comcast.net.

Sue lives in New Jersey with her husband Bob and their dog, Oreo.

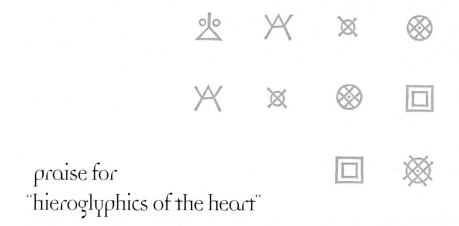

praise for
"hieroglyphics of the heart"

"Poems are the magic of life — Sue Lawley's even more so. Her poems cover the sweep of life from birth to death in loving, provocative and always accessible ways that enrich your own life."

— **Dr. Robert Akeret**
Author of *Tales From A Traveling Couch* and
Family Tales, Family Wisdom

"These heartfelt poems by the gifted Sue Lawley embody the spirit of over-coming life's challenges with wisdom, enlightenment and compassion. This inspirational read is especially suited for those in the midst of reinvention or anyone searching for a deeper meaning to their everyday struggles. You won't be disappointed!"

— **Sue Frederick**
Author of *I See Your Dream Job: A Career Intuitive Shows You
How to Discover What You Were Put on Earth to Do* (St. Martin's Press)

"Susan Marc Lawley's *Hieroglyphics of the Heart* is full of nuggets of wisdom gained through a life well lived. These poems are moving and rooted in the details of one woman's story and they bring alive the people she loves."

— **Maria Mazziotti Gillan**
American Book Award Winner for *All That Lies Between Us*

Words failed; what did family mean?/
It would take a lifetime/to answer these questions.

"So writes Sue Lawley in this illuminating collection of poems reflecting generations of stories from one Italian-American family. We relish the old

continued

ways of *pasta drying on chair backs and bedspreads* and *the rooster in the claw foot tub;* we are taken to a new life in a sixteen room manor house; we grieve as one after another of the beloved family departs; we understand that possessions do not fulfill the narrator's yearning, so she turns to her work: *I feel something more precious than crown jewels.// I feel useful in the world/.* And finally we witness the affirmation of the writer as artist, finding the way of deeply healing, in community: *And when the credits roll,/most leave/but the writers stay,/ reading/...all the letters/that/scroll/ away.* This moving book illuminates every corner it explores; it is light shed by a storyteller, who is a poet."

— **Patricia Lee Lewis**
Patchwork Farm Retreats; *A Kind of Yellow*

"This is what I predict: that you the reader will read all of the poems in Sue Lawley's collection in one gulp. That you will read some of them twice, memorize at least two, and send favorite ones to all your friends.

I predict that you will recognize the narrator of these poems as much as you would recognize an old friend: the woman who realizes that today she has lived one day longer than her mother; the woman whose house speaks up when it is told it is soon to be sold; the woman whose husband bookends each of her days 'with kindness'; the woman whose grandfather chose not to win the clam-eating contest out of compassion for his friends who needed the prize money more.

These poems reach across the time of a life, and the life of that time. You will read less about events, however, than about the inner life of the woman experiencing the events. You will hear the soft admission that, 'There is comfort in things that do not change in drastic ways.' You will recognize the emotion of loss when things *do* change in drastic ways on the compelling pages of Sue Lawley's fine book."

— **Eunice Scarfe**
Saga Seminars; IWWG Instructor